ISBN-13 978-1545575338

Printed in The United States of America

The Extravagant Letter X

Coloring Book

By Peggy Louise Parrish

C.2017

Welcome to the letter X . This book is full of creative forms of the letter X. Take out your colors and have fun inside these pages. It is recommended that you use a high quality colored pencil. However, markers, paints and watercolor pencils can also be used on these pages if you place a scrap paper under your page.

This book is just one book of the lettering books of artist Peggy Louise Parrish. She calls her lettering "Letter Wonders". There are examples of coloring to copy for some of the X letters. The real fun is in choosing your own coloring,

Perhaps you need a fancy letter X for some reason. Think of the words six, box,taxes, relax, fox, exhibit,exit and ax.

Hopefully you will have some fun on these pages. Please keep the initials of the artist PLP on each page. Feel free to make a few in house copies of any pages that you would like to try in different colors. Give away or exhibit your coloring of these letters.(Please do not sell any of your coloring pages for a profit) Make some X letters for yourself after you finish. If you like this book, all the letters of the alphabet have books by this artist.

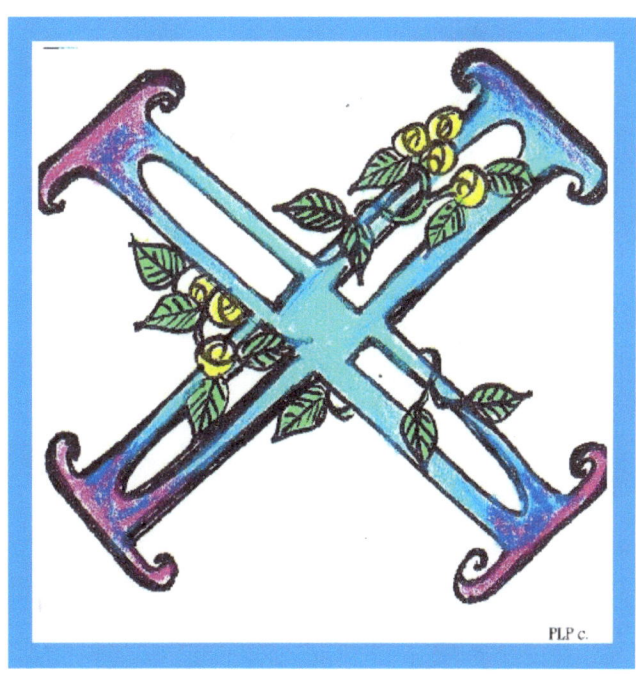

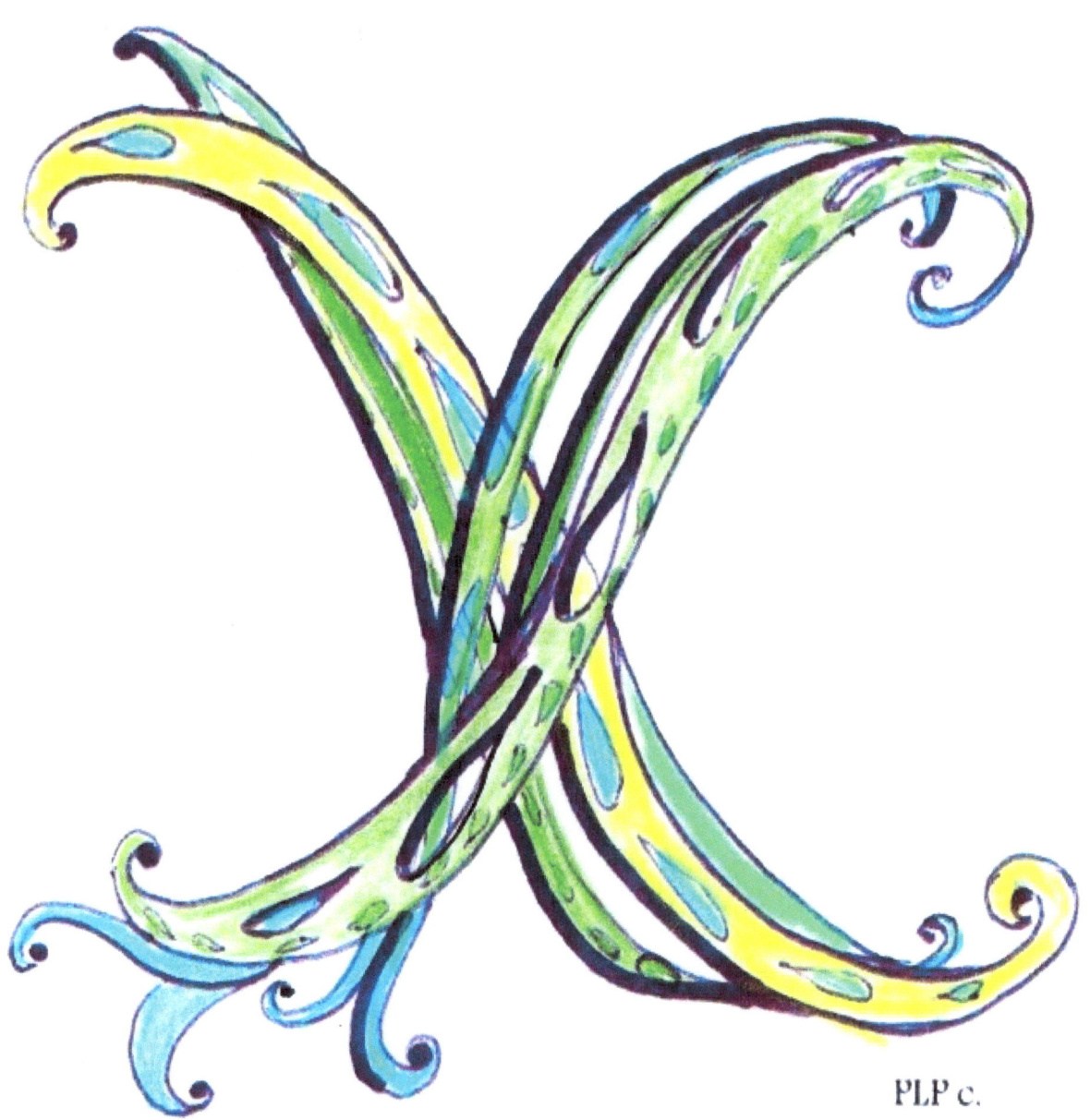

PLP c.

7

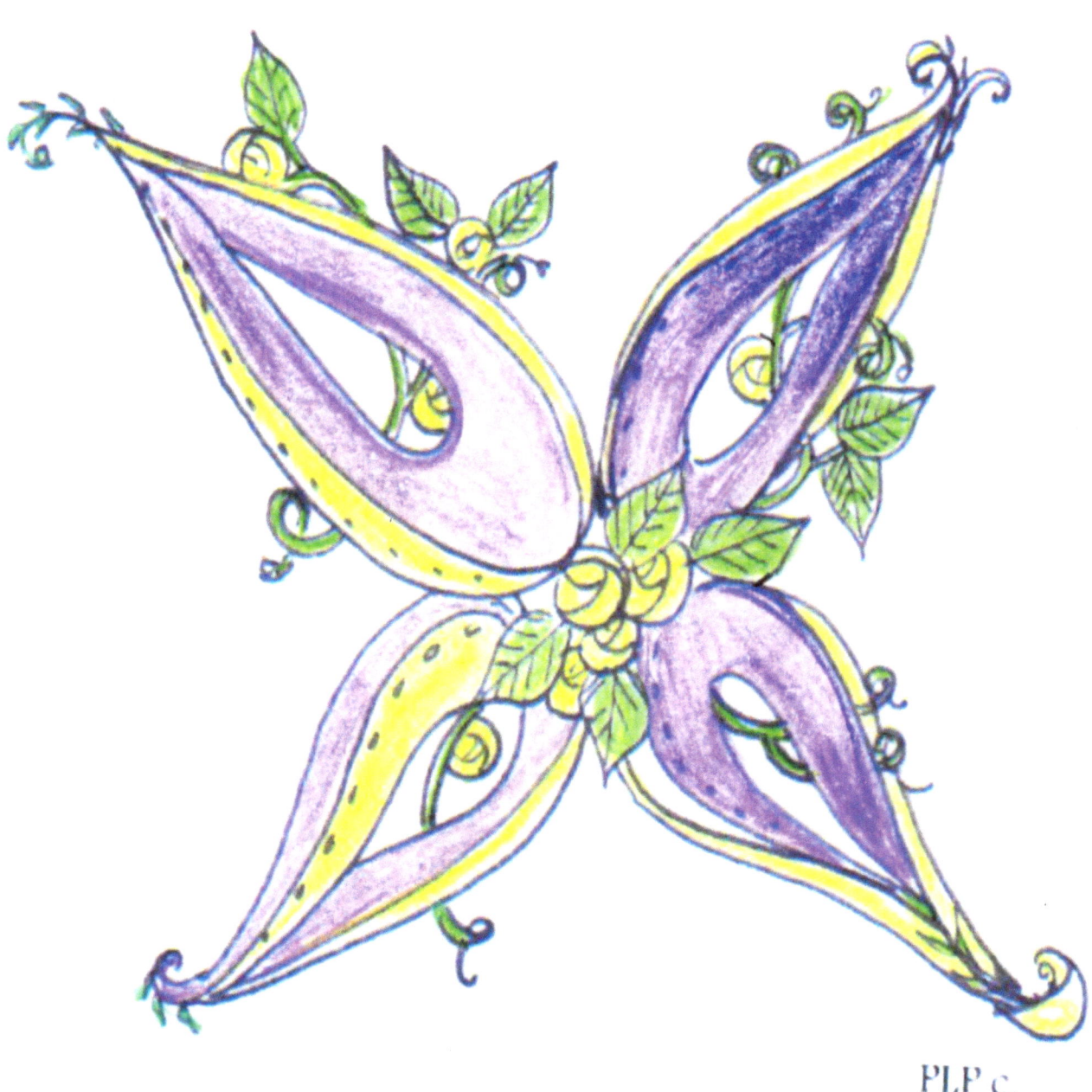

PLP c.

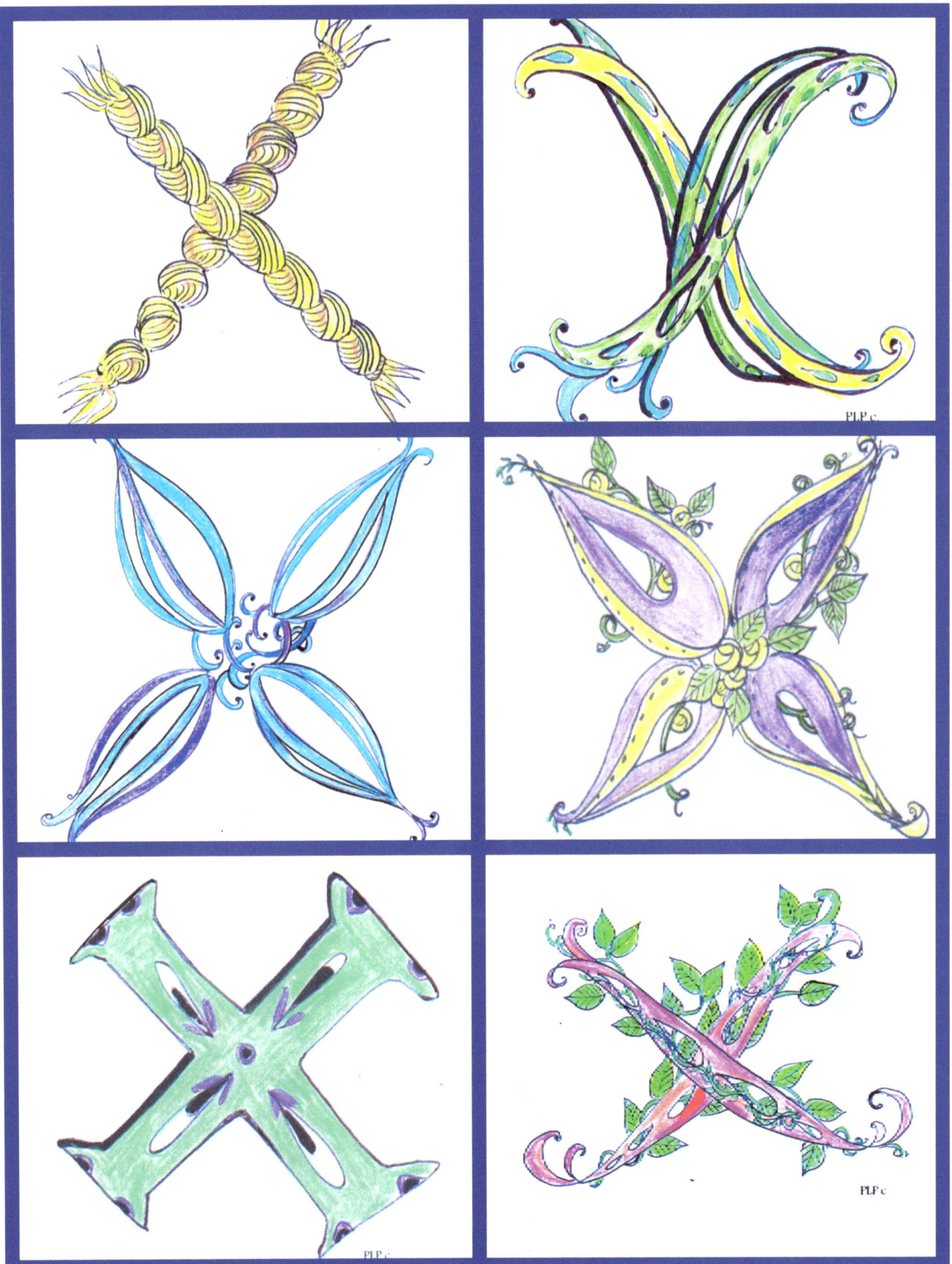

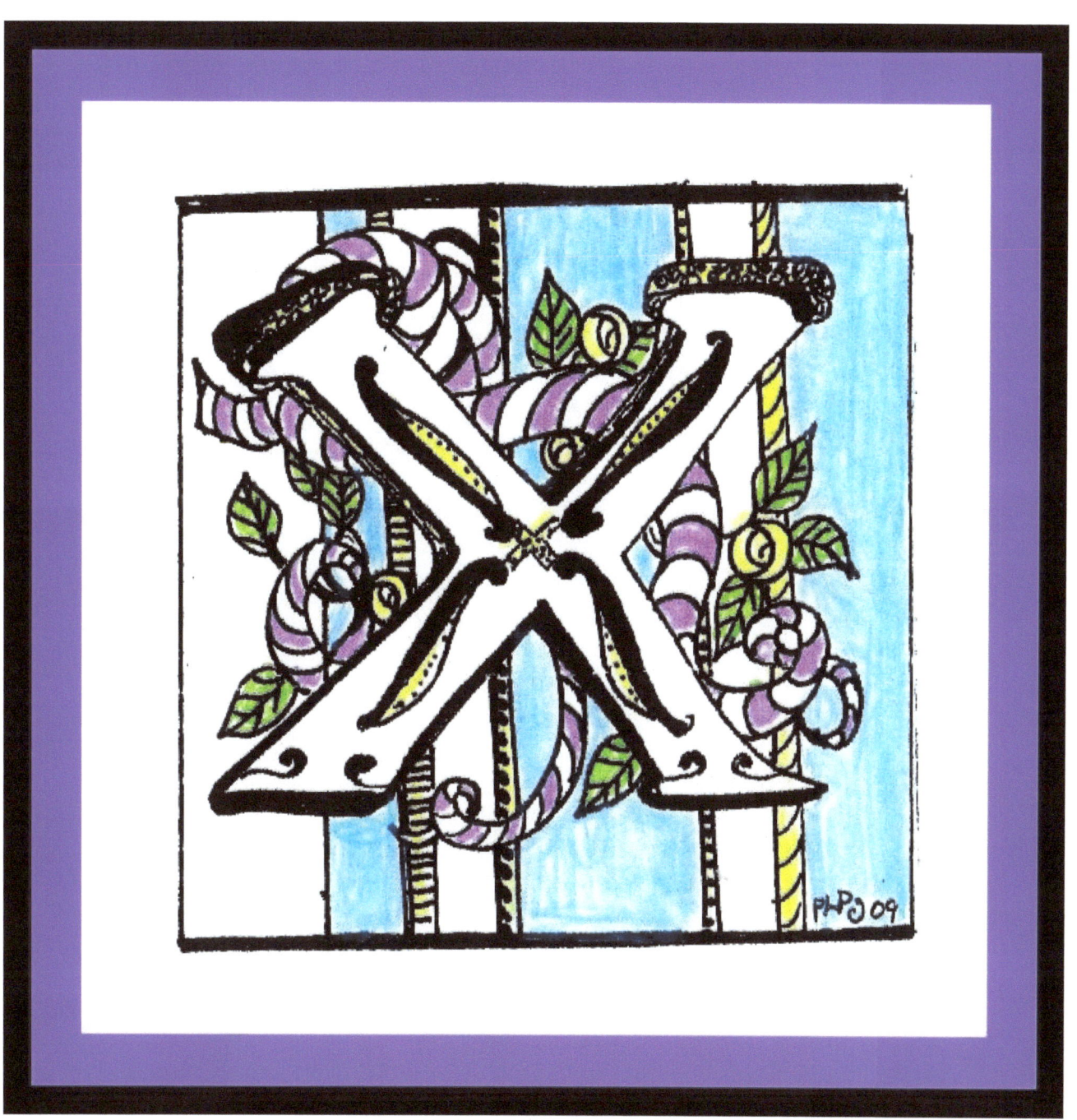

13

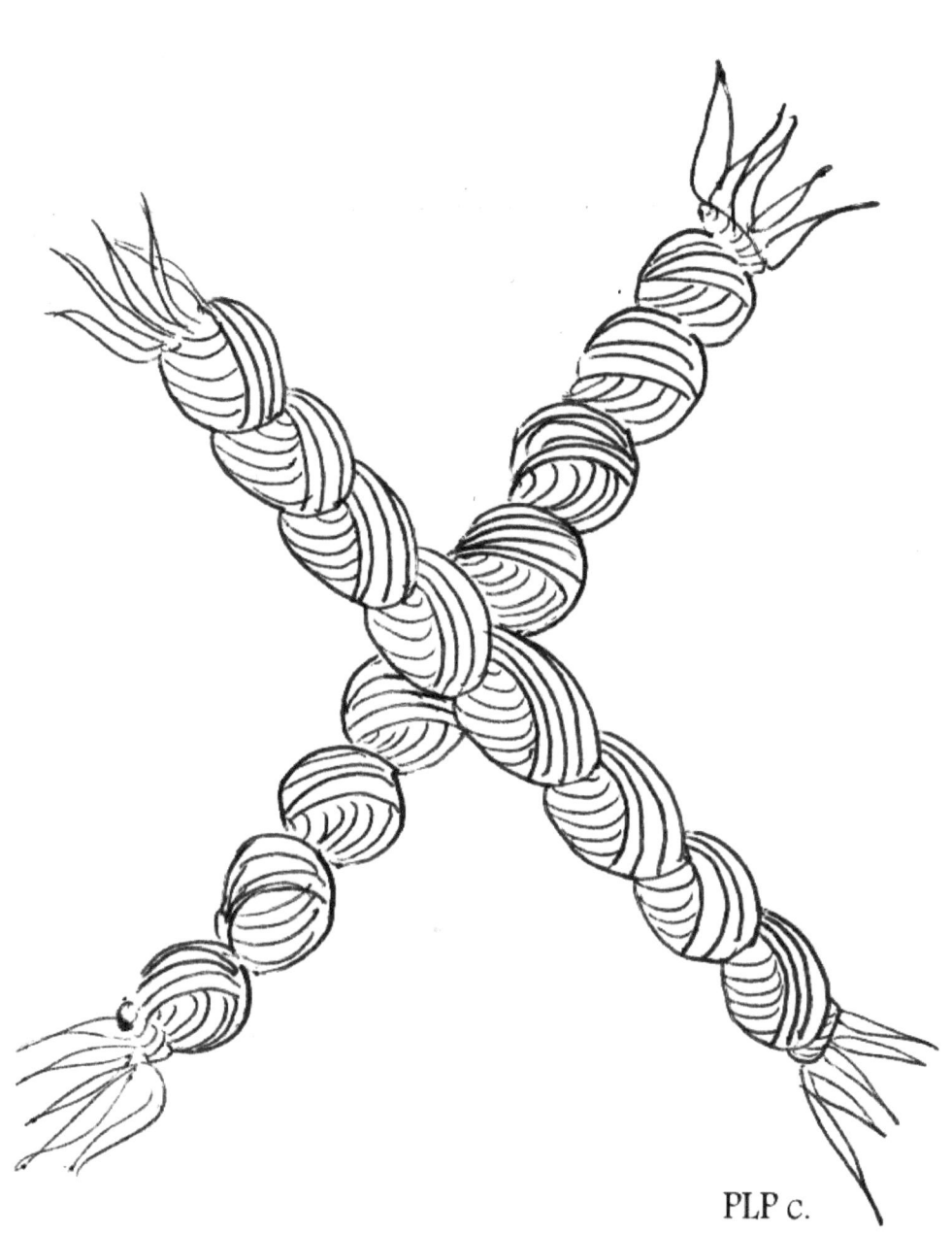

PLP c.

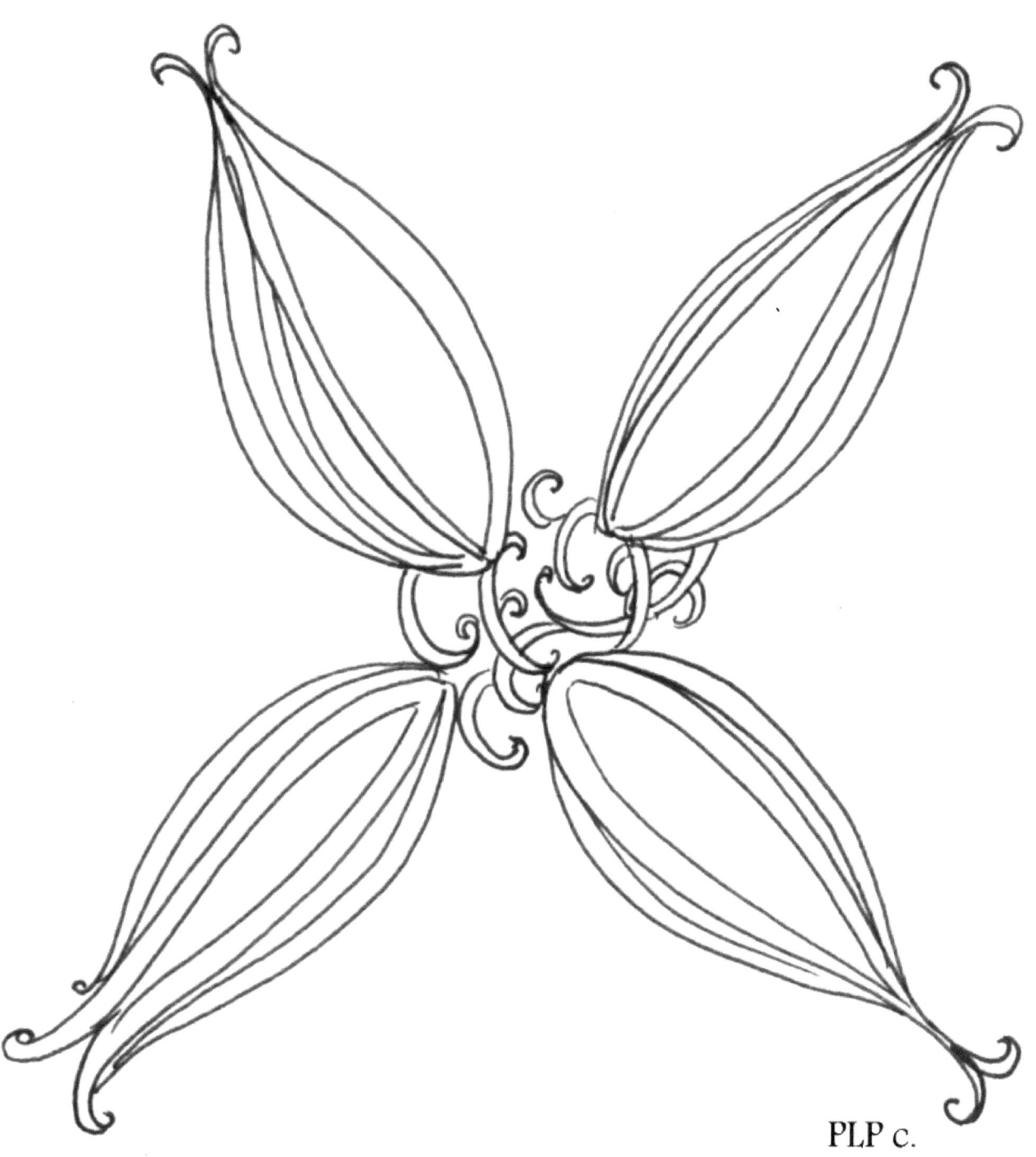

PLP c.

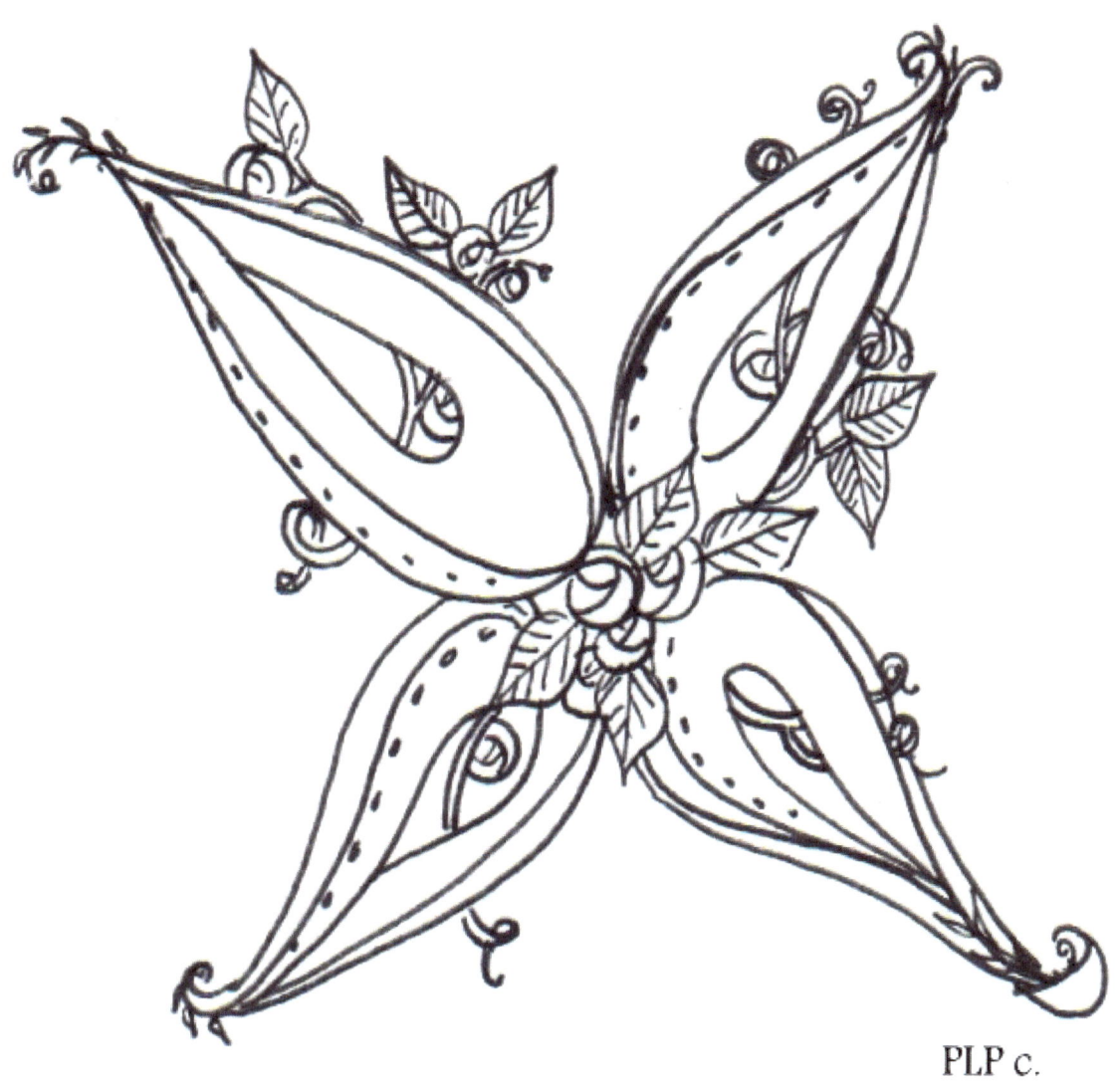

PLP c.

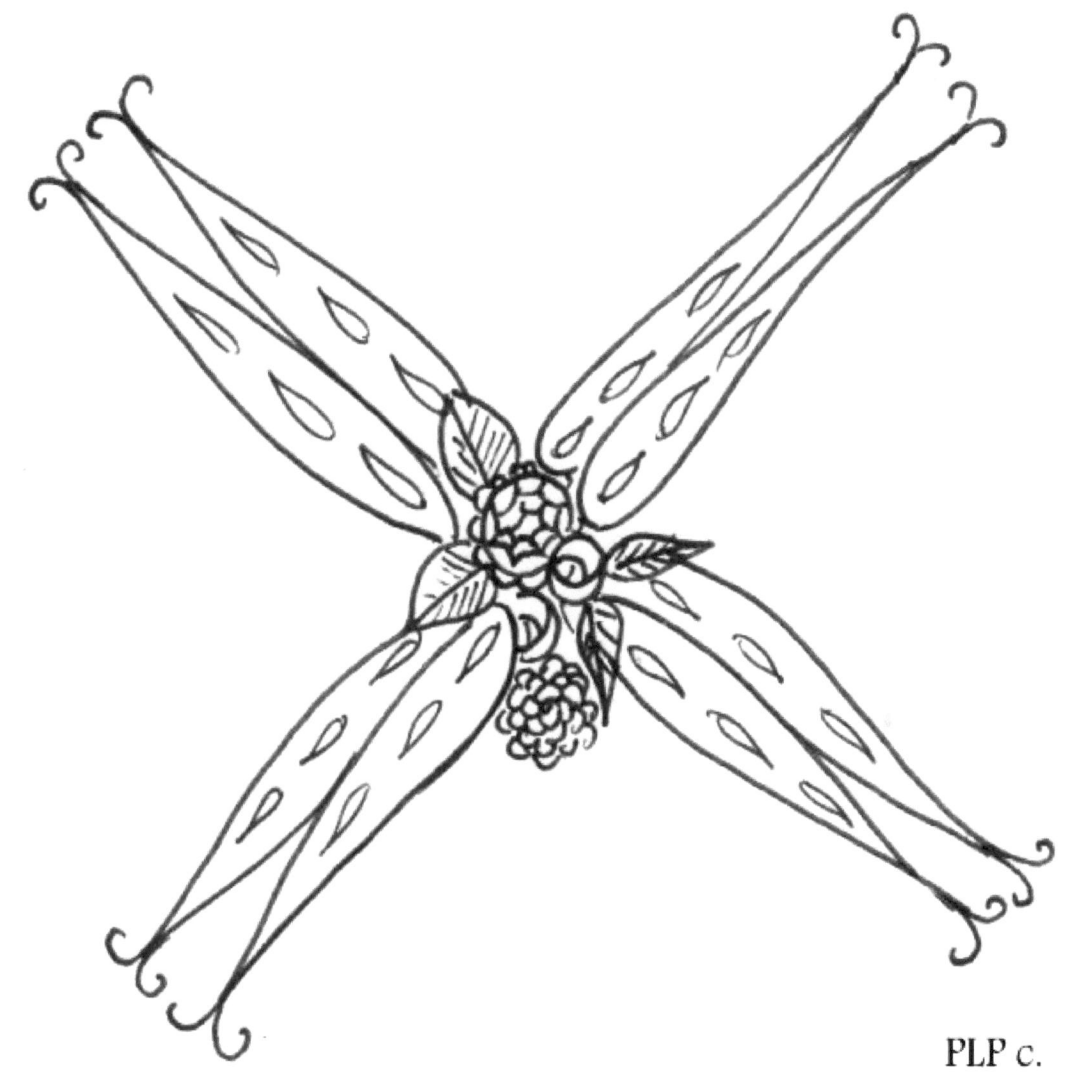

PLP c.

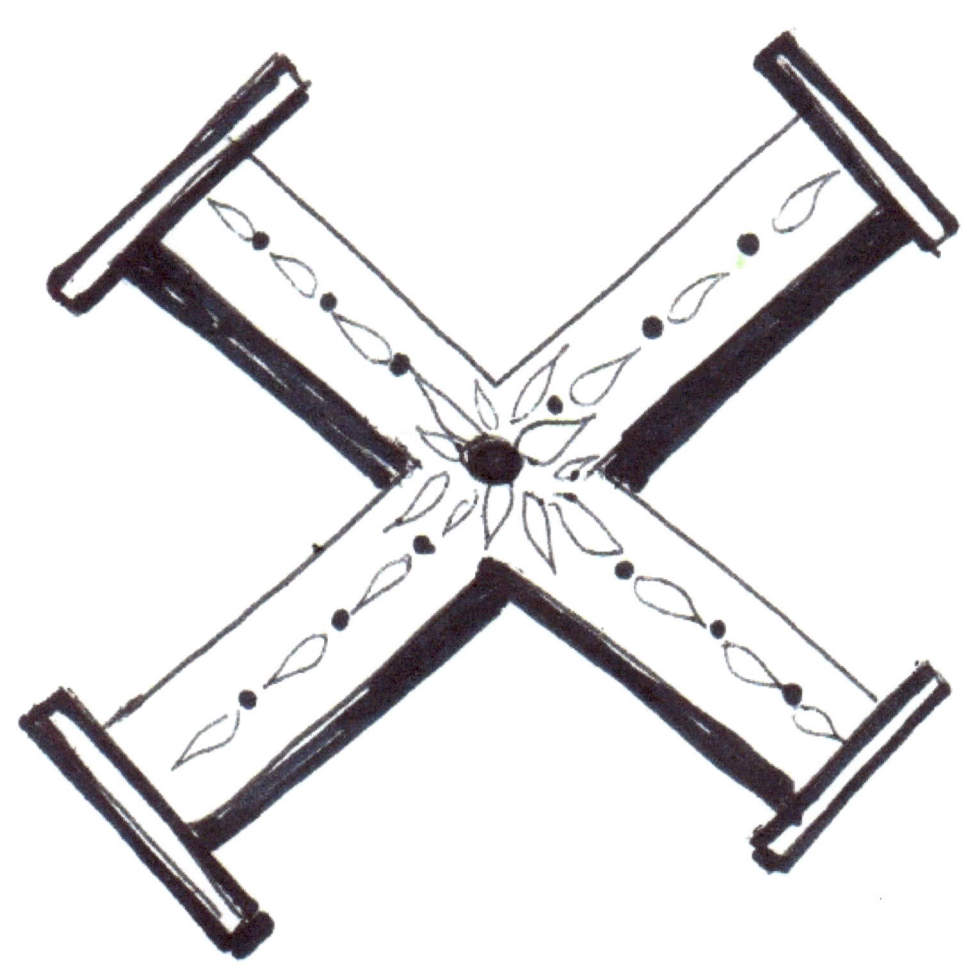

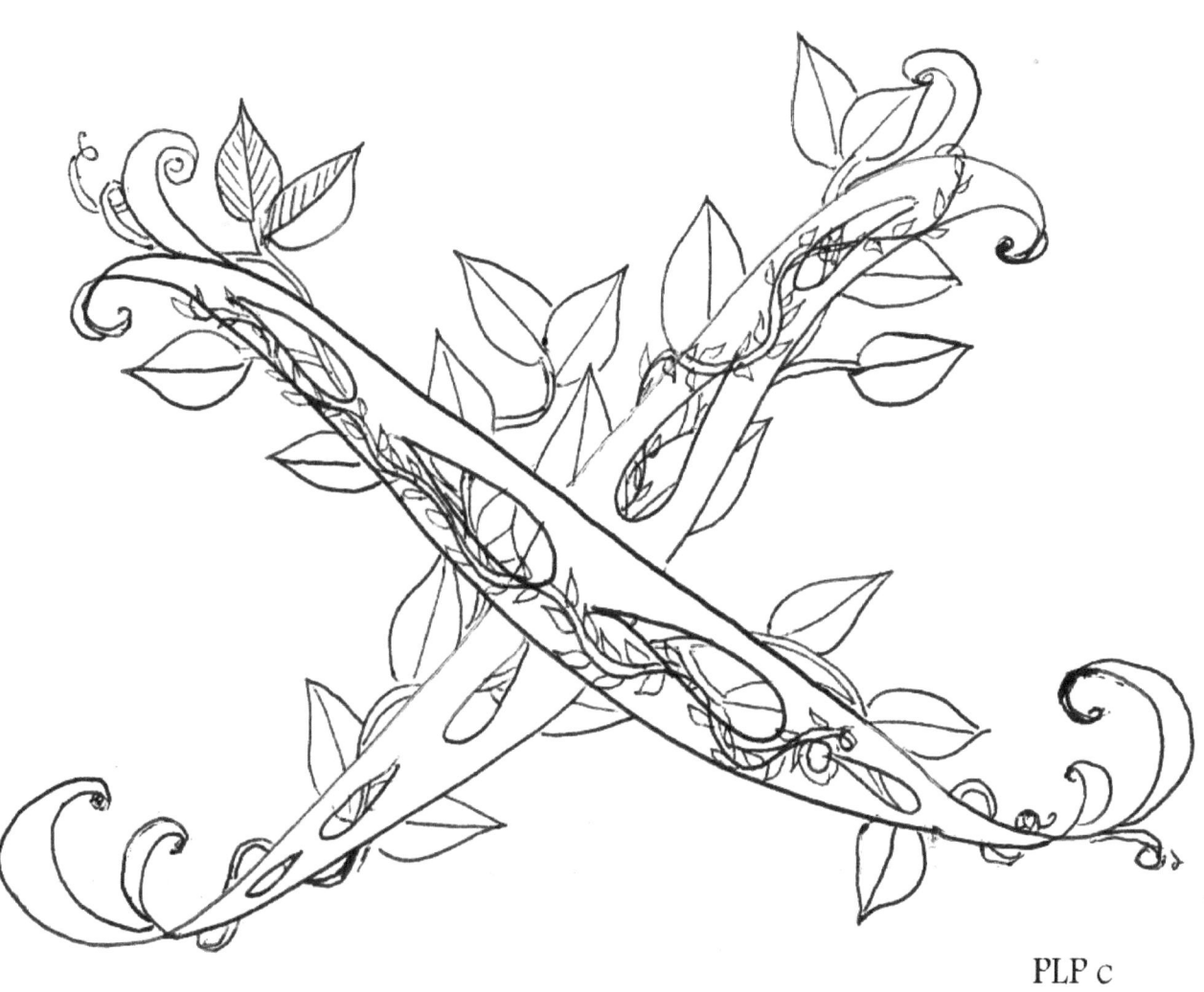

PLP c

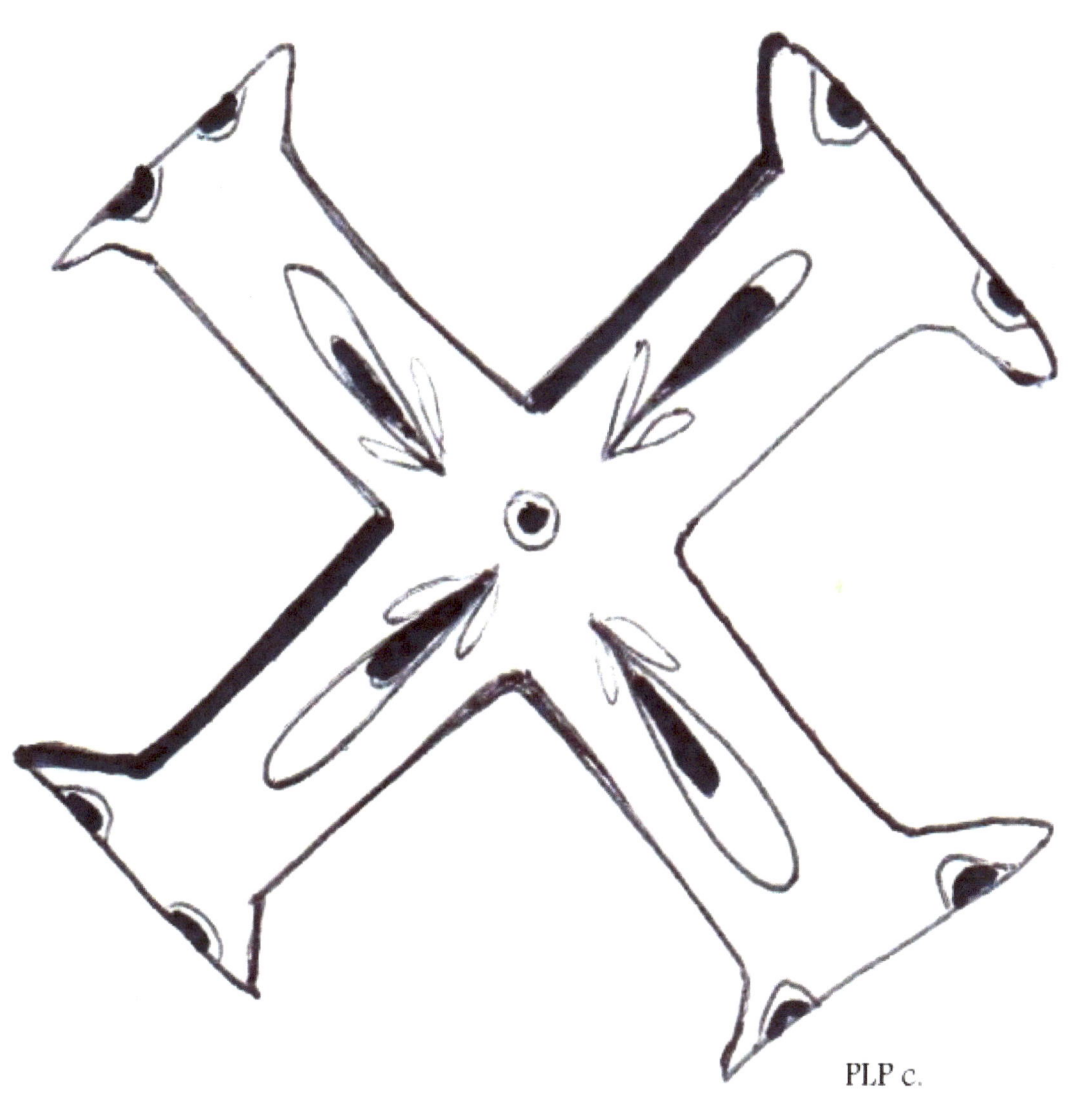

PLP c.

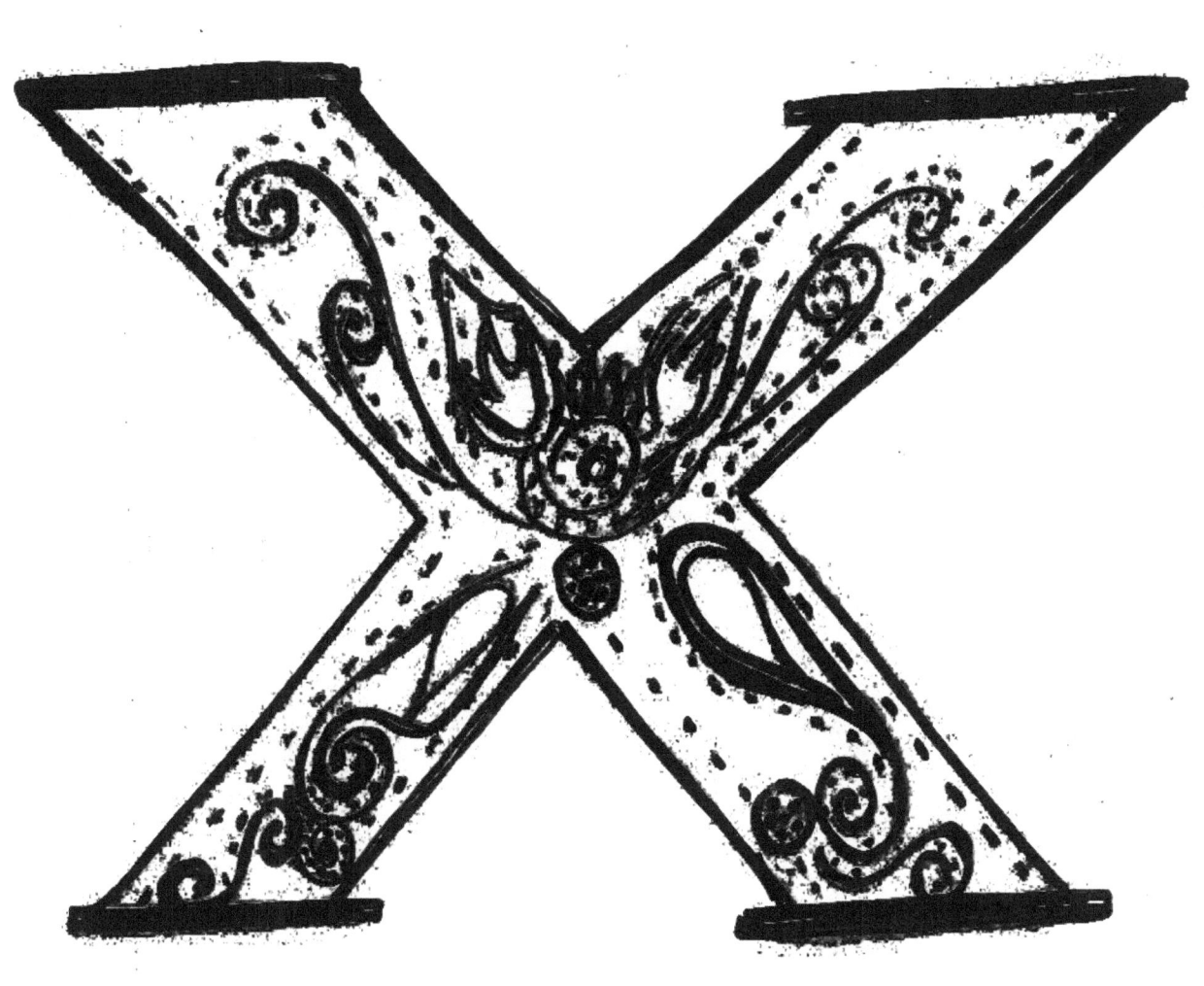

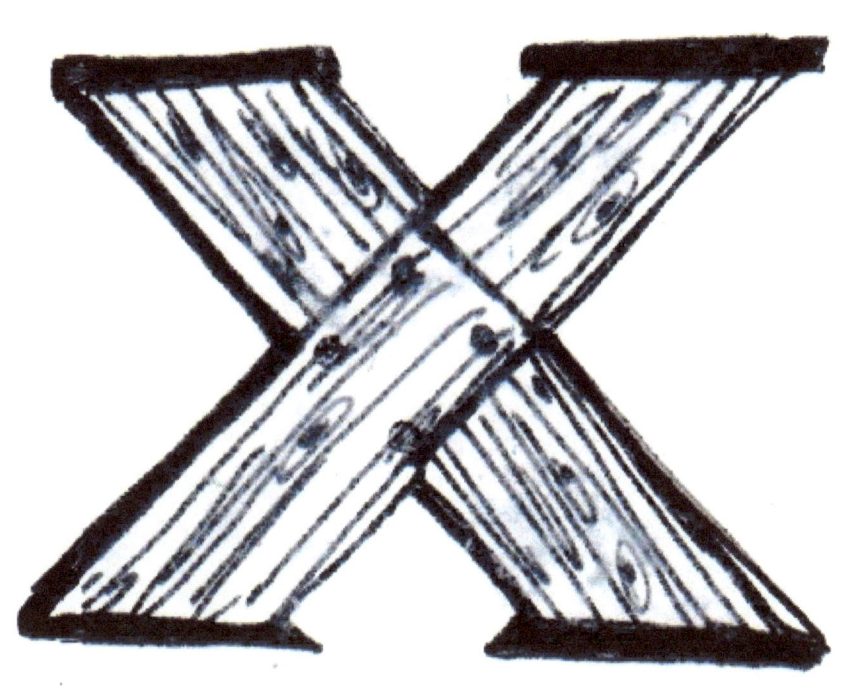

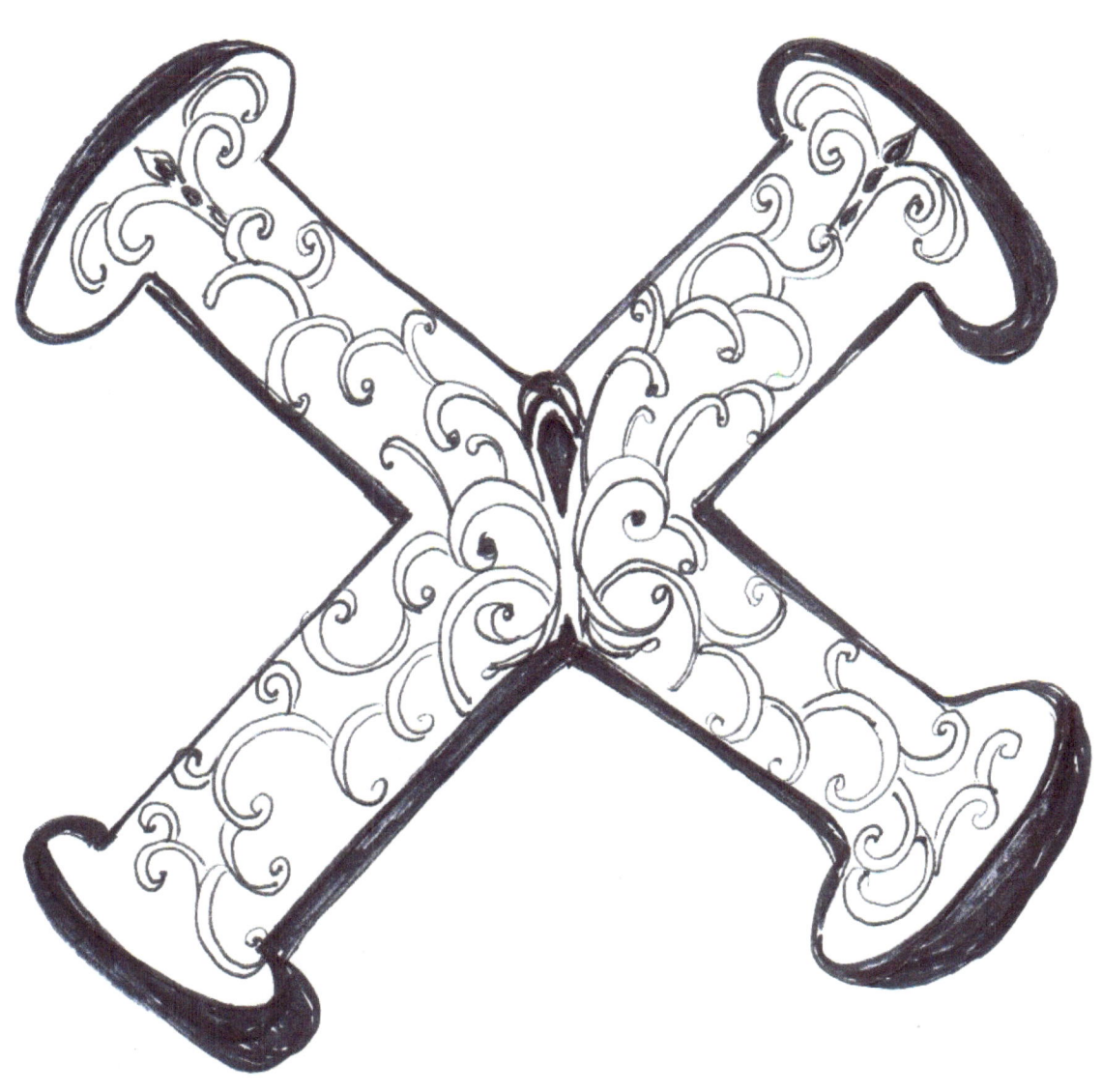

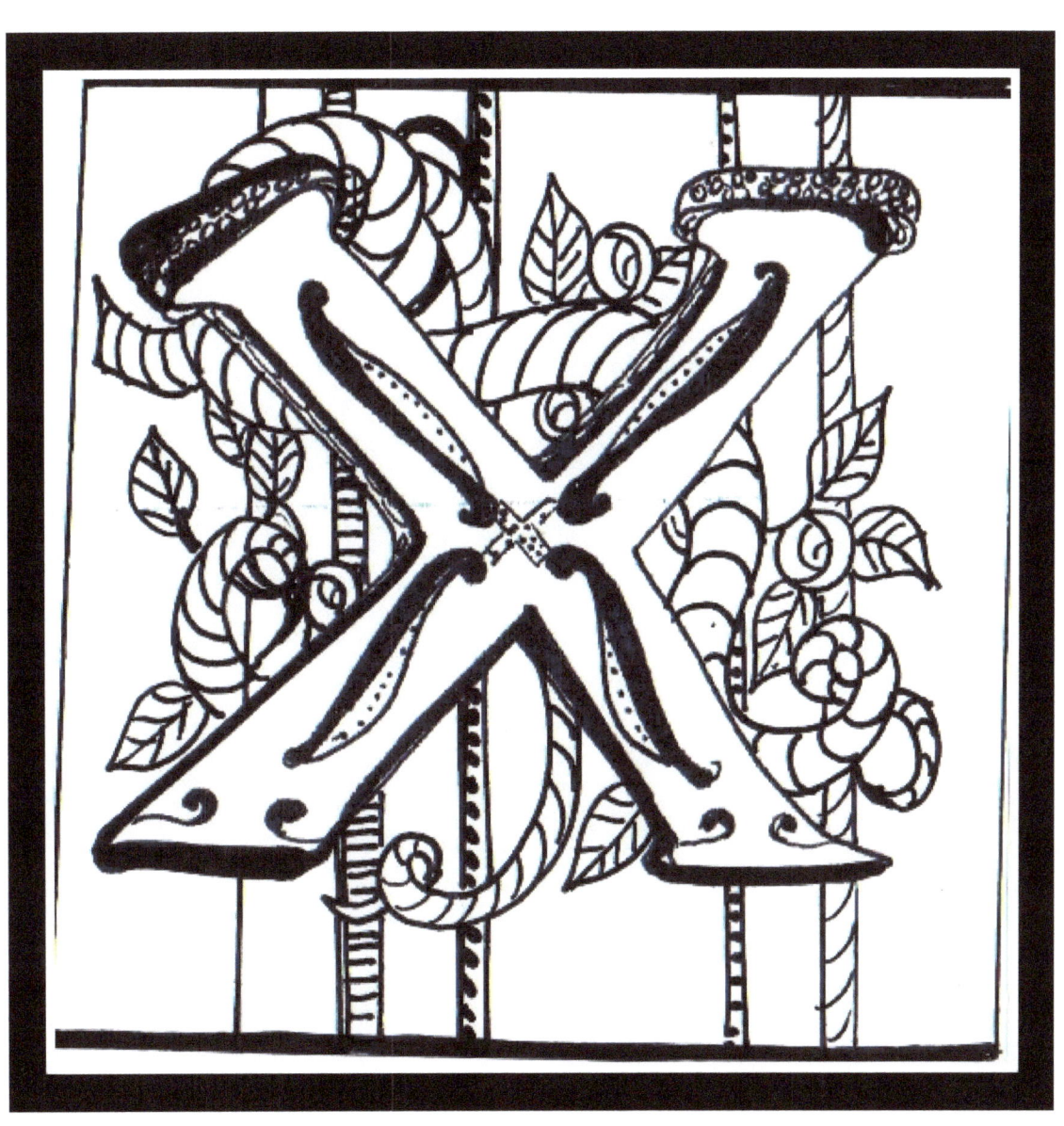

PLP c.

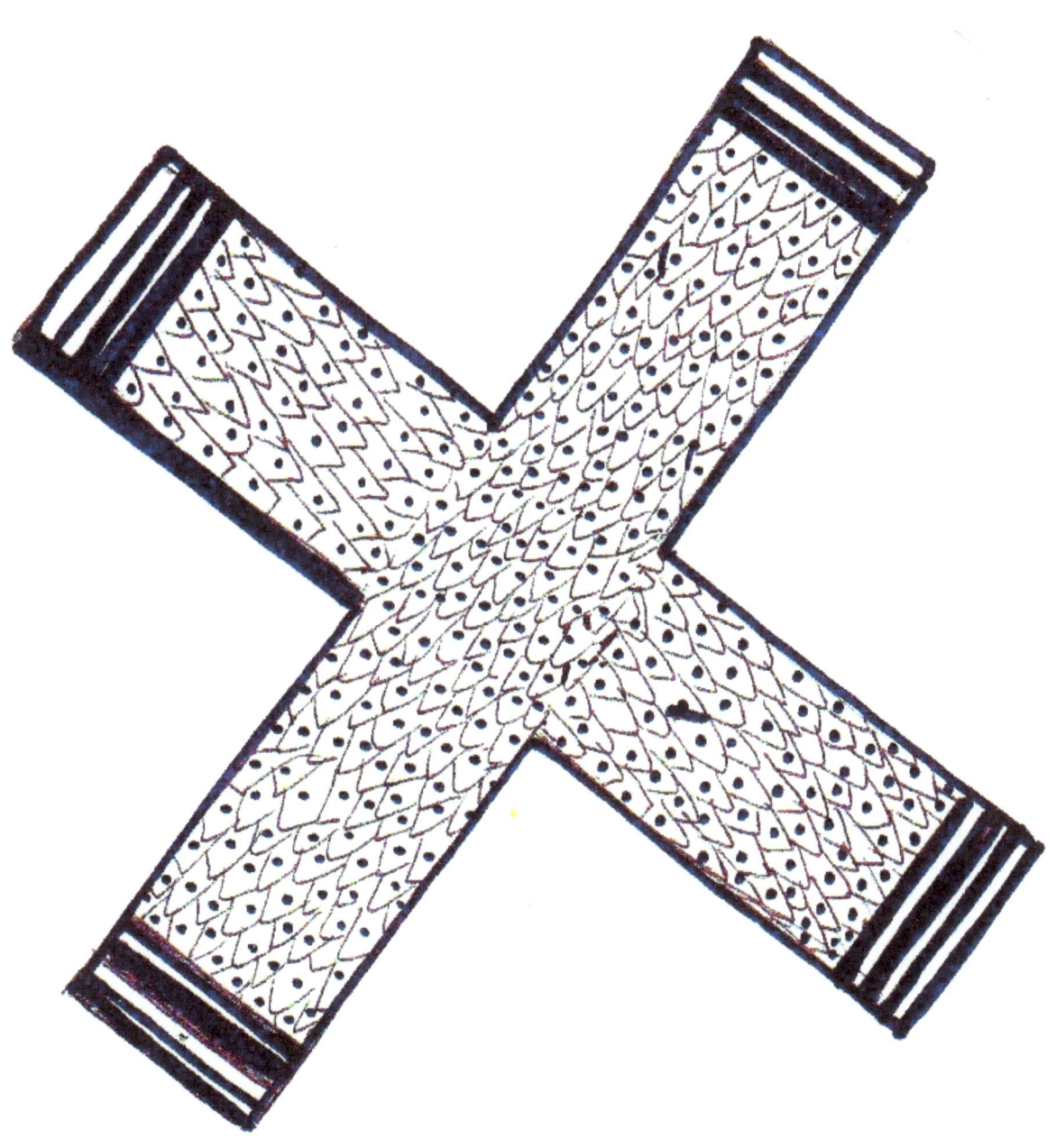

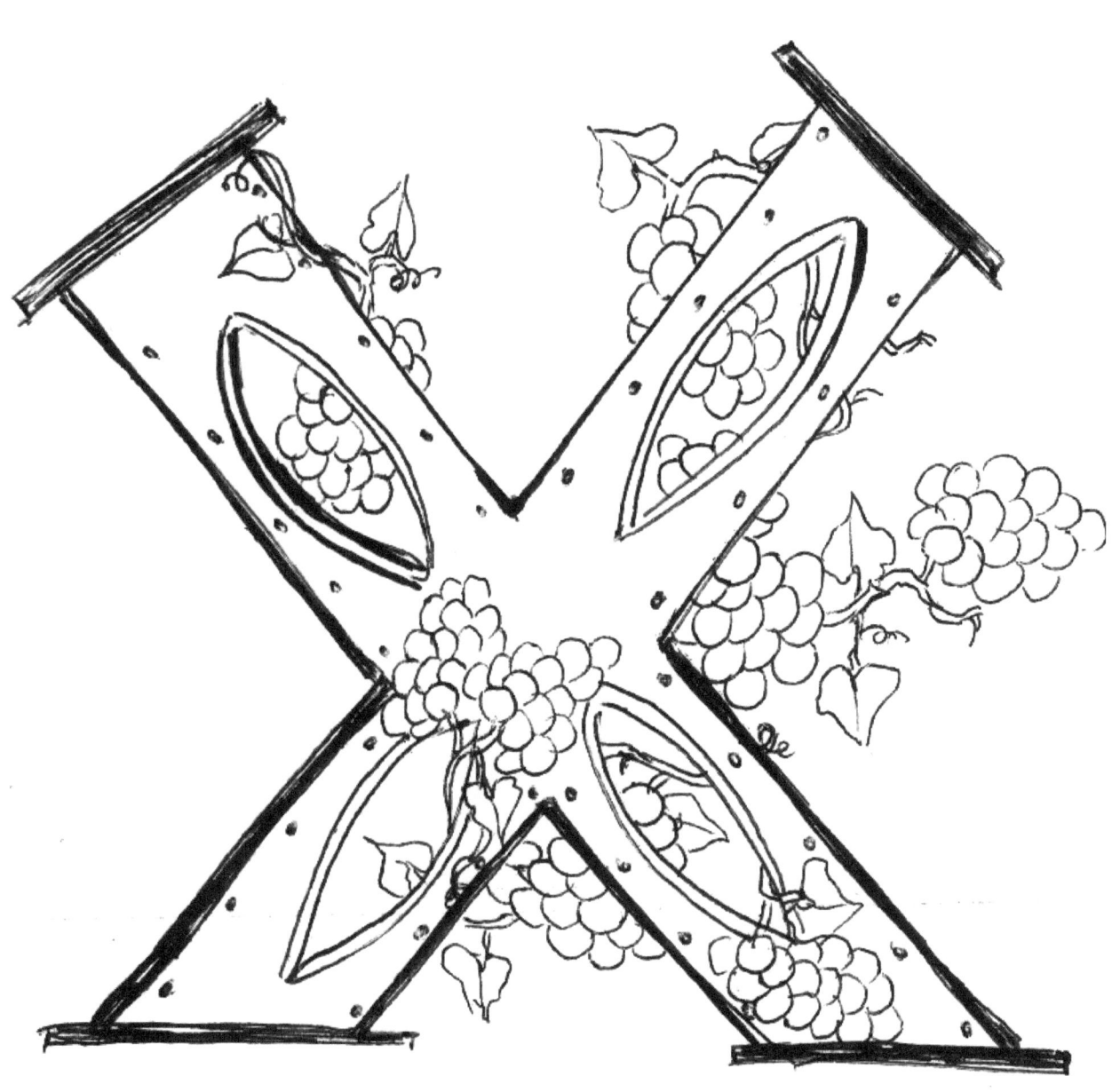

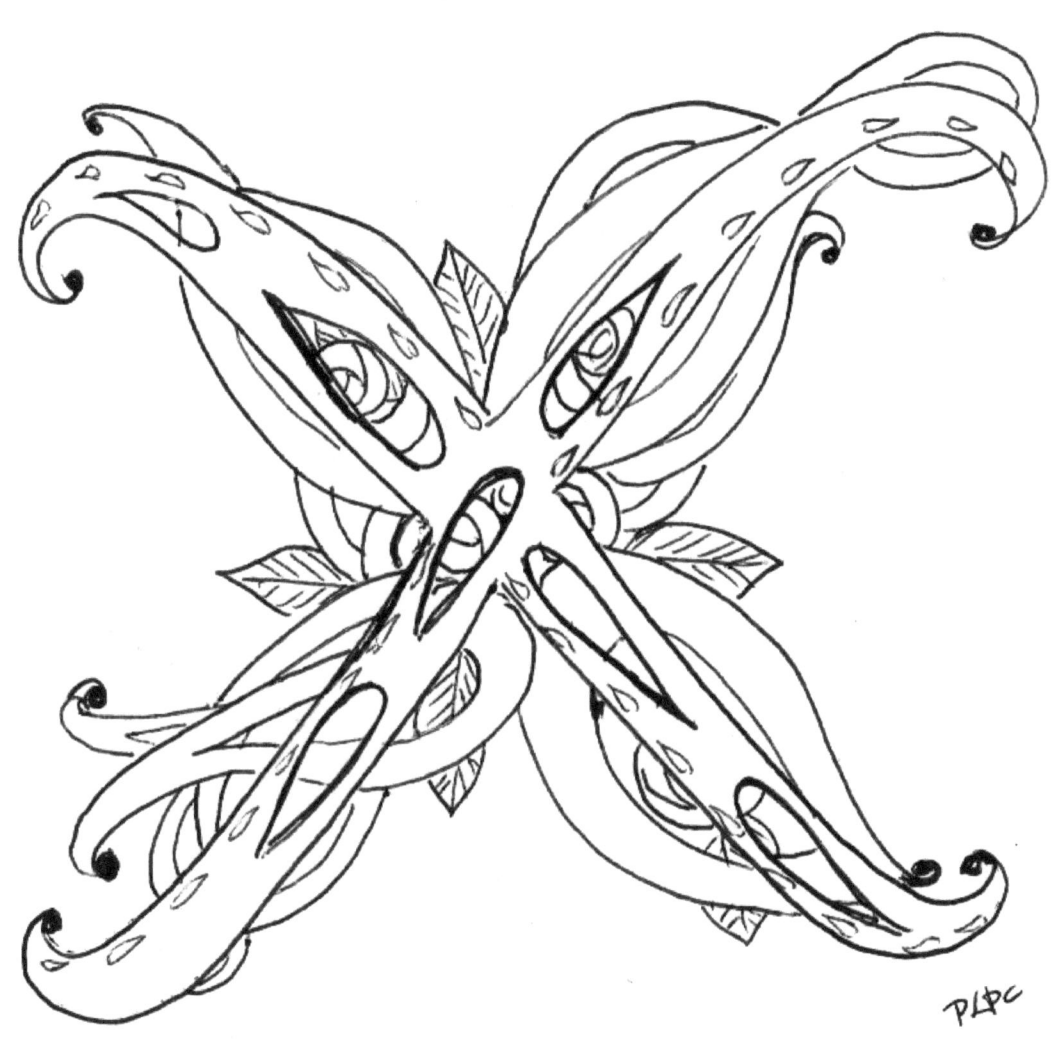

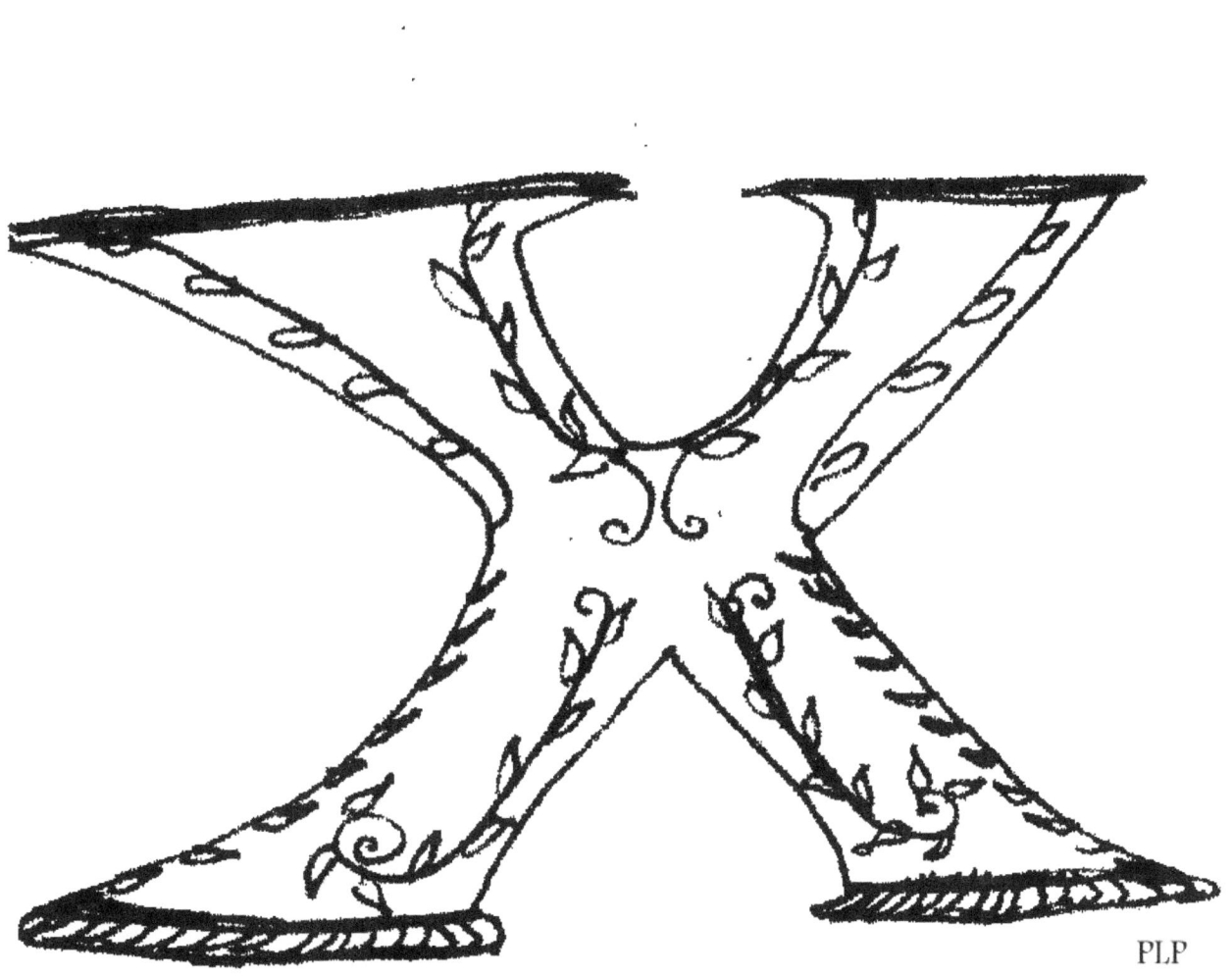

PLP

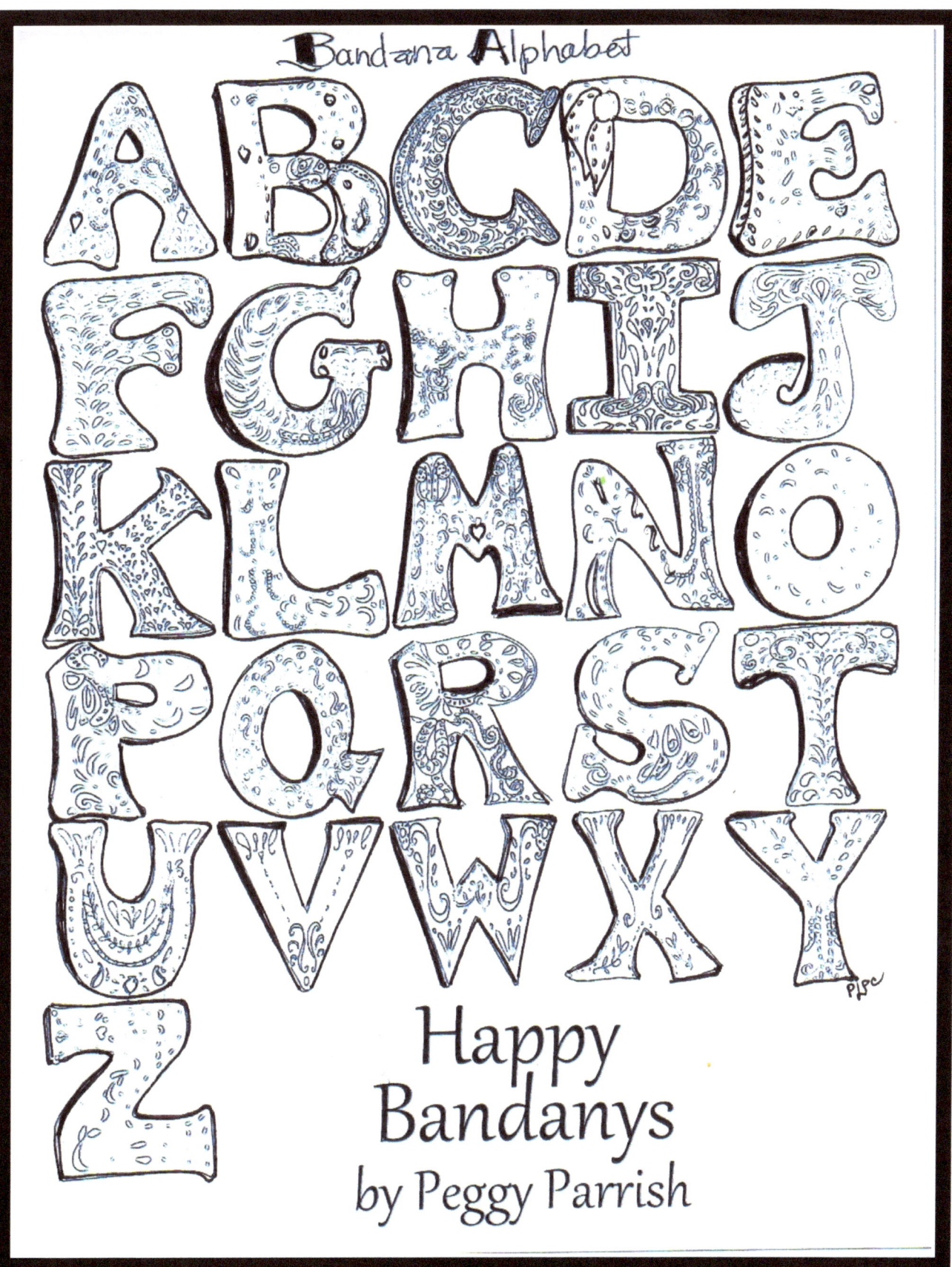

Bandana Alphabet

Happy
Bandanys
by Peggy Parrish

Letter x fits in every alphabet nicely. It is actually a very important letter and symbol. Why not try to make some of your own. The Bandana letter X and it's alphabet look best done with a marker with a small tip and a scrap paper under your work. Leave the little shapes white(without color). Use marker around the shapes. You will be surprised how cute your bandana letter X will look.

Its fun to look around in this world and find the letter X. Are there usually 2 letter Xs under a picnic table? Where else can you find X?

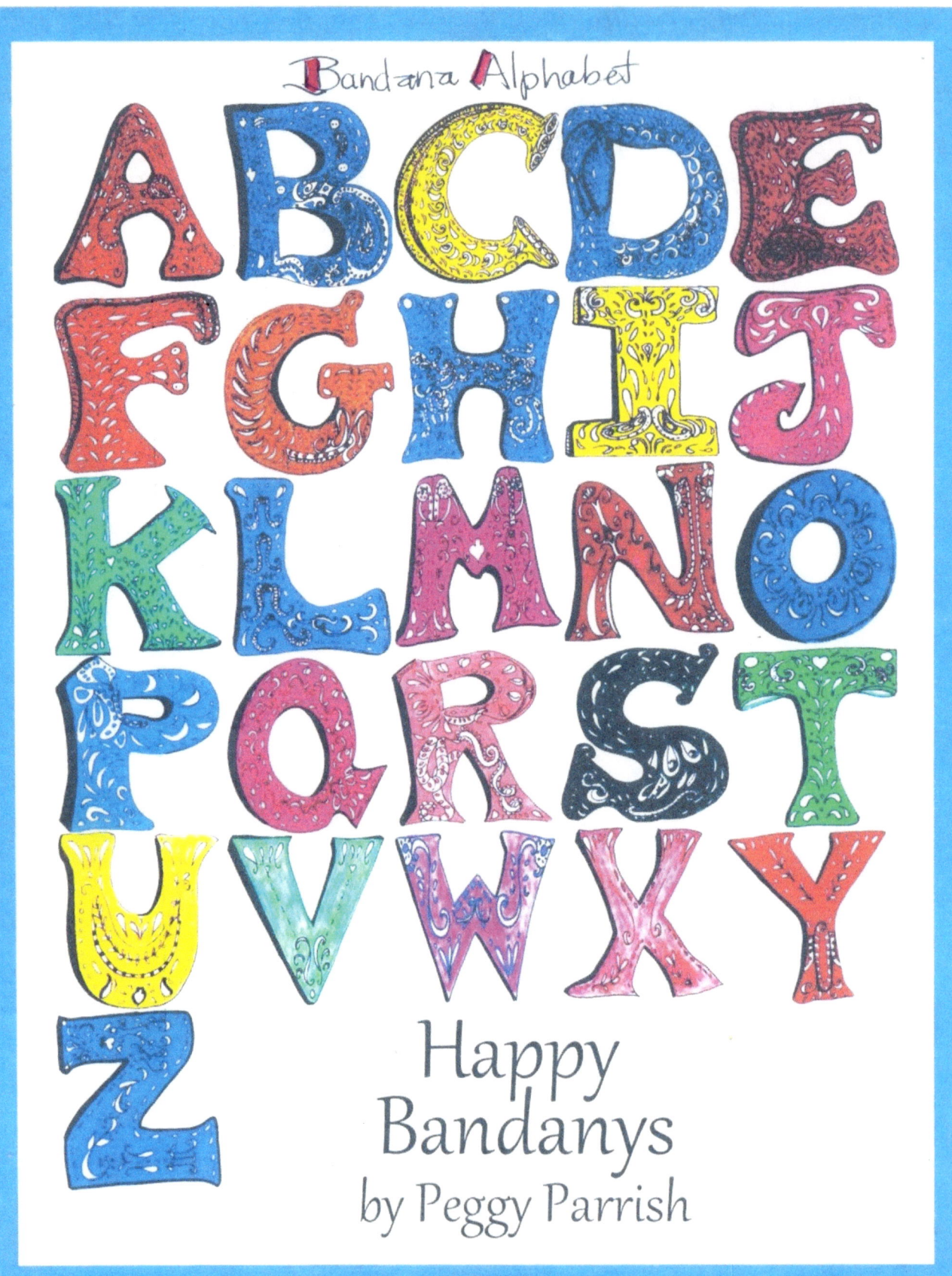

Bandana Alphabet

Happy
Bandanys
by Peggy Parrish

56

www.ingramcontent.com/pod-product-compliance
Lightning Source LLC
Chambersburg PA
CBHW051052180526
45172CB00002B/615